WORKBOOK

For

The Value of Others:

Understanding the Economic Model of Relationships to
Achieve and Keep More of What You Want in the
Sexual Marketplace

Stanley Powers

i

Table of Contents

HOW TO USE THIS WORKBOOK

Welcome to Orion Taraban's The Value of Others workbook companion. The purpose of this workbook is to give you a methodical way to go deeper into the content of the book. With the help of key chapter summaries, highlighted key takeaways, self-reflection questions, life-changing exercises, and self-evaluation prompts, it seeks to help you comprehend the economic model of relationships.

The Value of Others: Understanding the Economic Model of Relationships to Get (and Keep) More of What You Want in the Sexual Marketplace by Orion Taraban is a book that this workbook is meant to supplement. It is meant to be a helpful tool to help you explore and apply the text's principles, not a replacement for it. Use this workbook in conjunction with the main text to gain a thorough understanding.

Guidelines for Using the Workbook

- Chapter Summaries: Every chapter summary in The Value of Others offers a condensed synopsis of the main ideas and points raised in that chapter. Utilize these synopses as a fast reference or to brush up on your knowledge prior to beginning the workbook exercises.

- Key Takeaways: After reading the synopsis of each chapter, make a note of the key points that really struck a chord with you. These realizations may serve as stimulants for additional reflection and application of the book's ideas to your own life.

- Self-Reflection Questions: After every chapter summary, there are questions for self-reflection designed to encourage contemplation and a more thorough examination of your experiences and ideas regarding relationships and values. Take your time thinking through these questions, and for clarity, you might want to write down your responses.

- Life-Changing Exercises: This workbook contains a range of activities that are based on the concepts taught in The Value of Others. These activities are designed to support personal development, self-awareness, and empowerment while assisting you in putting the book's concepts into practice. Choose exercises that resonate with you and incorporate them into your daily routine for lasting change.

- Self-Evaluation Questions: At the end of the workbook, you will find self-evaluation questions to assist you in tracking your progress and growth as you apply the concepts from the book. Use these questions to reflect on your achievements, identify areas for improvement, and set goals for future personal development.

4

OVERVIEW

A practical and occasionally contentious examination of interpersonal relationships in general and romantic and sexual relationships in particular can be found in Orion Taraban's book The Value of Others: Understanding the Economic Model of Relationships to Get (and Keep) More of What You Want in the Sexual Marketplace. He views partnerships as exchanges of value, utilizing ideas from economics to investigate how individuals bargain for their place in the "sexual marketplace."

The central tenet of Taraban's thesis is that interpersonal exchanges of value, whether romantic or not, may be used to understand relationships. According to his theory, people in relationships are constantly weighing the value they may add to and derive from others, just like in any other type of business dealing. According to Taraban, this dynamic controls a lot of human behavior in romantic situations because people are continuously trying to maximize their personal benefits and get the greatest "deal" for themselves.

One of the main points of the book is that romantic relationships are a component of a market, or what Taraban calls the "sexual marketplace," in which individuals are always attempting to find their place and have values of their own. A person's attractiveness, personal power, social capital, and other people's perception of their desirability all play a role in this market. Within this perspective, individuals are seen as commodities whose values change according to both internal and external assessments. This method differs from more sentimental or conventional perspectives of relationships, which hold that love and emotional ties are the primary motivators.

The widely accepted notion that love is the most significant component of relationships is contested by Taraban. Rather, he contends that bargaining, power, and attraction are the main forces behind human connections. He contends that individuals are constantly attempting to obtain the best possible outcome in terms of emotional fulfillment, companionship, and even sexual fulfillment by negotiating to improve their surroundings. These discussions are essential to human relationships because they influence how individuals establish and nurture their connections throughout time. The premise is that every relationship is a never-ending game of bargaining in which both partners strive to get the best possible deal for themselves.

Taraban's claim that power dynamics are present in all relationships and that the more powerful party always prevails in these talks is among his more contentious statements. According to him, partnerships are rarely really equal, with one partner frequently having more influence than the other, much like business transactions. In this context, power can originate from a variety of places, including social standing, physical attractiveness, material prosperity, mental stability, or even the capacity to control or emotionally affect another individual. According to Taraban's reasoning, those in positions of greater authority typically have the upper hand when it comes to setting the parameters of a relationship, including its limits, emotional exchanges, and general course.

According to Taraban, one of the main sources of power in the sexual marketplace is attractiveness. He underlines how having physical attractiveness, charm, and social appeal can significantly increase one's market value and provide attractive people more negotiating power in romantic relationships. Taraban contends that attractiveness is more than just physical appearance; it's about the whole package, which includes a person's personality, charm, and social skills. This idea may sound simplistic. The ability to negotiate favorable terms in relationships and one's position in the sexual hierarchy are determined by their attractiveness in conjunction with other forms of power.

Taraban challenges the idea of "happily ever after," claiming that it is a myth, in keeping with his economic model. He contends that relationships are dynamic and never fully satisfying. They are dynamic, ever-changing as people change and as the value they offer to one another varies. This viewpoint presents a sobering image of relationships as dynamic contracts that require constant renegotiation. According to Taraban, relationships cannot be guaranteed to be happy or sustained indefinitely without ongoing attention to the shifting dynamics of power and value.

The notion that relationships' real dynamics have little to do with love, as it is commonly understood, is arguably one of the book's most provocative ideas. According to Taraban, people enter into relationships for reasons other than love—namely, the advantages they stand to receive. He believes that romantic love is a myth that is frequently used to cover up the fact that relationships are fundamentally transactional. He contends that people remain in relationships because they gain something worthwhile from them, such as emotional stability, companionship, status, or other advantages, rather than just because they are in love. This is different from the idealized stories that are prevalent in popular culture, where love is viewed as the primary driver of relationship sustainability.

Furthermore, Taraban puts forth the notion that not every relationship is feasible. People may desire to create ties with certain others, but the reality is that relationship potential is limited by the worth each person perceives in the other. This economic framing emphasizes that although people may want to connect with certain people, the value that each person brings to the table limits how viable these connections can be. Furthermore, Taraban observes that there is always a "better move" available in relationships, meaning that individuals are continuously comparing their alternatives and determining whether there is a better deal they could be making, whether with their present partner or someone else.

The final chapter of the book tackles the premise that people, deep down, may not actually want partnerships in the way they anticipate. Taraban says that many persons are drawn to the notion of relationships but are not completely aware of the realities and complications required in maintaining them. He thinks that what people often crave is the emotional fulfillment and stability that relationships give, rather than the connection itself. This approach questions the premise that everyone is seeking meaningful, long-term connections, stating instead that people are motivated by their own needs and ambitions, which may not necessarily coincide with the idea of a committed partnership.

In essence, The Value of Others offers a novel and pragmatic vision of relationships through an economic lens. By presenting emotional and sexual encounters as transactions in a marketplace, Taraban encourages readers to rethink traditional concepts of love, attraction, and partnership. His concentration on power dynamics, negotiation, and value transfers provides a unique viewpoint on how relationships are formed, sustained, and eventually dissolved. While some readers may find his approach cynical or too analytical, the book definitely presents a thought-provoking exploration of the hidden mechanisms that govern human relationships in the modern world.

CHAPTER 1: THE MEDIA THROUGH WHICH VALUE IS EXCHANGED ARE RELATIONSHIPS

Chapter Summary

The first chapter discusses the concept of relationships as a transactional medium where value is traded between persons. According to Taraban, interactions in interpersonal relationships work similarly to exchanges in the marketplace, where people are always evaluating what they stand to gain and what they have to give. This viewpoint contradicts the conventional wisdom that says relationships are only emotional or motivated by love. Rather, the emphasis lies in how people assess their own and other people's worth, which results in a relationship where terms are constantly negotiated.

Key Takeaways

- In relationships, value is constantly evaluated and exchanged, much like in economic transactions.

- People assess their own and other people's value in relationships, which affects how they interact.

- The transactional aspect of human behavior frequently eclipses emotional bonds.

- Clarity on interpersonal interactions and expectations can be obtained by viewing relationships through this lens.

- Understanding that relationships are transactional can enable people to bargain for better terms for themselves.

Self-Reflection Questions

How can I assess my value in a relationship?

_____

_____

_____

_____

_____

What do I think I contribute to my relationships with others?

_____

_____

_____

_____

_____

In a relationship, have I ever felt taken advantage of? If so, how?

_____

_____

_____

_____

_____

When I believe that others do not value me, how do I respond?

_____

_____

_____

_____

_____

How can I better balance my expectations and needs in relationships?

_____

_____

_____

_____

_____

Life-Changing Exercises

Write down your strengths and what you bring to your relationships, focusing on both emotional and practical aspects.

Create a list of your past relationships and evaluate them based on how you perceived the value exchanged in each one.

Role-play negotiation scenarios with a friend, practicing how to express your needs and desires in a relationship.

Set personal boundaries that reflect your worth and ensure you communicate them clearly to others.

Reflect on a relationship that has ended; analyze what you learned about the value exchange that took place.

CHAPTER 2: SEXUAL RELATIONSHIPS ARE TRANSACTED IN THE SEXUAL MARKETPLACE

Chapter Summary

In this chapter, Taraban delves deeper into the concept of the sexual marketplace, where sexual relationships are viewed as commodities exchanged based on perceived value. He argues that individuals constantly assess their desirability and the desirability of potential partners. This assessment impacts their choices and the dynamics within relationships. Taraban emphasizes that understanding this marketplace allows individuals to navigate their sexual relationships more effectively, making informed decisions about who they engage with and why.

Key Takeaways

- The sexual economy runs on the idea that individuals judge desirability and value in possible partners.
- Sexual relationships are often transactional, where both parties seek to maximize their satisfaction and benefits.

- Understanding one's position in the sexual marketplace can empower individuals to make better choices regarding partners.

- The dynamics of desirability can shift dependent on several aspects, including social rank, looks, and personality.

- Awareness of these transactional aspects can lead to healthier and more fulfilling sexual relationships.

Self-Reflection Questions

How do I perceive my desirability in the sexual marketplace?

_____

_____

_____

_____

_____

What factors do I consider when evaluating potential partners?

_____

_____

_____

_____

_____

Have I ever felt undervalued in a sexual relationship, and what led

to that feeling?

_____

_____

_____

_____

_____

How do societal standards of attractiveness influence my choices in

partners?

_____

_____

_____

_____

_____

What changes can I make to better understand my role and value in the sexual marketplace?

_____

_____

_____

_____

_____

Life-Changing Exercises

Reflect on past sexual relationships; note how each relationship aligned with your perceived value in the marketplace.

Create a personal "value statement" that outlines what you believe you bring to the sexual marketplace.

Engage in discussions with friends about their perceptions of the sexual marketplace and compare your insights.

Write down the qualities you find most attractive in others and assess how those traits align with your personal values.

Investigate various cultural viewpoints on relationships and sexuality to increase your comprehension of the sexual marketplace.

CHAPTER 3: IN THE SEXUAL ECONOMY, EVERY INDIVIDUAL IS VALUABLE

Chapter Summary

According to Taraban, the worth of an individual in the sexual marketplace is based on a variety of criteria, including personality, emotional intelligence, social position, and physical appeal. This chapter explores the idea that value is dynamic and subject to change in response to external factors as well as individual growth. Taraban places a strong emphasis on realizing one's intrinsic worth and how self-improvement can increase it. People are empowered to look for relationships that reflect their worth as a result of this realization, which promotes healthier relationship dynamics.

Key Takeaways

- Each person has a distinct worth in the sex industry, which is shaped by a variety of personal characteristics.

- Value is fluid; it can change in response to one's own development as well as external events.

- Acknowledging one's intrinsic worth is essential to creating wholesome and satisfying relationships.

- A person's standing in the sexual marketplace can be improved through personal growth and self-awareness.

- Respect for one another and more harmonious relationships are fostered by acknowledging the worth of others.

Self-Reflection Questions

How do I evaluate my worth in a sexual relationship?

_____

_____

_____

_____

_____

Which qualities, in my opinion, increase my value in the sex market?

_____

_____

_____

_____

_____

Have I made any efforts to increase my sense of worth? If so, what improvements have I seen?

_____

_____

_____

_____

_____

Do I appreciate the worth of others and how do I respond to their values?

_____

_____

_____

_____

_____

How can I develop my worth to draw in better relationships?

_____

_____

_____

_____

_____

Life-Changing Exercises

Make a plan for your personal growth that outlines your objectives for improving your abilities and qualities.

Make a list of the attributes you value in other people and consider how you may develop such qualities inside yourself.

Take part in activities like public speaking or artistic expression that help you feel more confident and good about yourself.

Seek feedback from trusted people about your strengths and places for improvement on your value in relationships.

Remind yourself of your value and worth in the sexual marketplace by practicing self-affirmations.

CHAPTER 4: EVERYBODY IS ATTEMPTING TO HAGGLE FOR THE BEST DEAL THEY CAN

Chapter Summary

The final chapter highlights the premise that everyone in partnerships is engaged in a type of bargaining, aiming to acquire the greatest possible deal for themselves. According to Taraban, knowing how to negotiate can have a big impact on how relationships work out and help people more successfully express their needs and wants. He talks about different negotiating techniques and how to use them in romantic and sexual relationships, emphasizing the value of open communication and respect for one another throughout the process.

Key Takeaways

- In relationships, people always haggle and try to make the best bargain possible.

- More rewarding and happy relationships can result from having effective negotiating skills.

- In order to explain demands and aspirations during negotiations, clear communication is crucial.

- Gaining an understanding of negotiation strategies can help people improve their relationships.

- Effective bargaining in interpersonal interactions requires mutual respect and attention.

Self-Reflection Questions

To what extent do I feel at ease expressing my demands in relationships?

_____

_____

_____

_____

_____

Which tactics do I usually employ in partner negotiations?

_____

_____

_____

_____

_____

In what way did I react if I ever felt like my needs weren't met in a relationship?

_____

_____

_____

_____

_____

How can I enhance my communication abilities to facilitate better negotiations?

_____

_____

_____

_____

_____

What actions can I take to guarantee that my talks are civil and fruitful?

_____

_____

_____

_____

_____

Life-Changing Exercises

With a friend, run through bargaining scenarios, paying close attention to how you express your wants.

To help with future talks, make a list of the needs you have for your relationship and rank them.

Try out several negotiation tactics by role-playing them to determine which ones seem most logical and successful.

Think back to a recent negotiation in your life and evaluate what went well and what could have been done better.

Make a communication strategy that specifies how you want to communicate your needs and wants in relationships going forward.

CHAPTER 5: THE ESSENTIAL GAME OF HUMAN CONNECTIONS IS NEGOTIATION

Chapter Summary

This chapter demonstrates that human interactions, especially those in partnerships, inherently include bargaining. According to Taraban, in order to achieve mutual happiness, there must be a continuous exchange of wants and desires in any partnership. By knowing the dynamics of negotiation, people can create limits and make wise decisions in their relationships. Taraban highlights that preserving equilibrium and respect in interpersonal dynamics is just as important to bargaining as accomplishing individual goals.

Key Takeaways

- Every human interaction needs negotiation since it affects satisfaction and results.

- It is necessary to comprehend the goals and needs of both sides in order to negotiate effectively.

- Balance is essential for healthy relationships, therefore when negotiating, all parties should feel appreciated and heard.

- Effective communication is essential for successful negotiating because it reduces miscommunication and animosity.

- Gaining negotiating abilities can improve interpersonal connections and result in more satisfying conversations.

Self-Reflection Questions

In relationships, how do I usually approach negotiation?

_____

_____

_____

_____

_____

What techniques do I employ to successfully express my wants and

desires?

_____

_____

_____

_____

_____

Have I ever disregarded someone else's requirements during a negotiation? If so, what happened as a result?

_____

_____

_____

_____

_____

How can I make sure that, as opposed to being competitive, my negotiations are courteous and cooperative?

_____

_____

_____

_____

_____

How can I strengthen my ability to negotiate in order to cultivate

more positive relationships?

_____

_____

_____

_____

_____

Life-Changing Exercises

Jot down a recent relationship negotiation event and evaluate what went well and what could have been better.

Engage in active listening exercises with a friend or spouse to improve your ability to communicate during negotiations.

To help you feel more comfortable expressing your wants and desires, role-play negotiation scenarios.

Make a list of the boundaries that are unassailable in your relationships and make sure that everyone knows what they are.

Think back to a successful negotiation you have had in the past and note the elements that made it happen.

CHAPTER 6: THE STRONGER PLAYER IN THE GAME ALWAYS PREVAILS

Chapter Summary

When discussing the dynamics of power in relationships, Taraban emphasizes that the more powerful party frequently sets the parameters of participation. Domination is only one aspect of power; other aspects include emotional intelligence, self-assurance, and the capacity to persuade. The results of relationships can be greatly impacted by one's understanding of their own and other people's power. Rather than just tipping over to those who appear more dominating, this chapter urges readers to develop their own strength to build stronger, more harmonious relationships.

Key Takeaways

- Power dynamics are important in relationships because they affect how people behave.

- Usually, the more powerful person establishes the parameters for discussion and interaction.

- Power can take many different forms, such as confidence, emotional intelligence, and social standing.

- A person's ability to use their power and acknowledge it can result in more positive relationships.

- Maintaining a balance of power within a partnership helps foster mutual respect and understanding.

Self-Reflection Questions

What is my understanding of my own power in relationships?

_____

_____

_____

_____

_____

How do I view power dynamics affecting the way I interact with

other people?

_____

_____

_____

_____

_____

When was the last time I felt helpless in a relationship, and what happened?

_____

_____

_____

_____

_____

How can I strengthen my own influence to build relationships that are more harmonious?

_____

_____

_____

_____

_____

What techniques can I employ to successfully manage power dynamics in my relationships?

_____

_____

_____

_____

_____

Life-Changing Exercises

Think back to a previous relationship in which power dynamics were present and consider how it impacted the way things worked out.

Determine the spheres of your life in which you feel in control, then think about how to use that influence in your interpersonal interactions.

Make a vision board that embodies the traits and characteristics that add to your individual strength.

Take part in exercises that increase your self-worth and confidence, including assertiveness classes or public speaking.

Ask reliable people for their opinions on your power dynamics in relationships.

CHAPTER 7: ATTRACTIVENESS IS THE KEY TO POWER IN SEXUAL INTERACTIONS

Chapter Summary

In this chapter, Taraban delves into the idea that appearance plays a big role in determining power dynamics in romantic partnerships. He contends that physical appearance affects one's perceived worth in the sexual marketplace and determines desirability. Although physical attractiveness is important, personality, charm, and emotional intelligence are all significant elements. People can improve their appearance and manage relationships more skillfully by realizing that attractiveness has multiple facets.

Key Takeaways

- Beauty has a big impact on power dynamics in romantic relationships.

- A person's personality and emotional intelligence are just as important as their physical beauty when determining their attractiveness.

- People in positions of authority are frequently seen as more attractive, which increases their attraction.

- Comprehending and nurturing diverse facets of attractiveness can improve the results of relationships.

- Healthy interactions can result from navigating sexual relationships with an awareness of attractiveness dynamics.

Self-Reflection Questions

What is my personal opinion of my own attractiveness in a sexual

relationship?

_____

_____

_____

_____

_____

Which qualities do I think make me more appealing to other people?

_____

_____

_____

_____

_____

Has my perceived beauty ever caused me to feel underappreciated or ignored?

_____

_____

_____

_____

_____

How can I concentrate on enhancing the non-physical parts of my attractiveness?

_____

_____

_____

_____

_____

How can I improve and recognize other people's beauty in my relationships?

_____

_____

_____

_____

_____

Life-Changing Exercises

Make a list of the attributes that, in your opinion, go beyond physical appearance to make someone beautiful.

Take part in activities like personal grooming or fitness that boost your self-esteem and confidence.

Find out what your friends think is attractive about you. Pay attention to both your personality and your physical attributes.

To increase your overall appeal, practice expressing your individuality and charm in social situations.

Consider a moment when you felt especially attractive, and consider the circumstances that led to that perception.

CHAPTER 8: HAPPILY EVER AFTER IS NOT POSSIBLE

Chapter Summary

Taraban closes the chapter by criticizing the notion of a "happily ever after" in partnerships. According to his theory, relationships need constant work, compromise, and adjustment. The idealized notion of a flawless, dispute-free union is unattainable and may cause disillusionment. Rather, more genuine connections might result from accepting the complexity and difficulties that come with being in a partnership. Instead of concentrating on idealistic results, this viewpoint encourages people to prioritize relationship resilience, progress, and communication.

Key Takeaways

- The notion of a "happily ever after" can cause people to have irrational expectations for their relationships.

- Healthy relationships need ongoing work, compromise, and adjustment.

- More genuine connections can be cultivated by accepting the complexity of relationships.

- People can become more resilient by realizing that obstacles are an inevitable aspect of relationships.

- Building enduring, satisfying relationships requires a focus on communication and progress.

Self-Reflection Questions

In my relationships, what does "happily ever after" mean to me?

_____

_____

_____

_____

_____

Which relationship obstacles have I encountered, and how have I handled them?

_____

_____

_____

_____

_____

How can I change my expectations such that my interactions are centered on development and flexibility?

_____

_____

_____

_____

_____

How can I encourage honest discussion about our problems with my partner?

_____

_____

_____

_____

_____

How can I strengthen my relationships' resilience so that I can deal with challenges more skillfully?

_____

_____

_____

_____

_____

Life-Changing Exercises

Consider a difficult time in your relationship and consider the lessons you can draw from it.

Make a list of reasonable expectations for your relationships that emphasize flexibility and growth.

Communicate your needs and expectations for the relationship with your spouse in an open and honest manner.

Take part in resilient-building activities, such stress-reduction or mindfulness.

Think about getting help from a therapist or counselor to examine relationship issues and create coping mechanisms.

CHAPTER 9: RELATIONSHIPS AND LOVE ARE UNRELATED

Chapter Summary

This chapter argues that although love is sometimes seen as the main driver of relationships, Taraban claims that love does not inherently determine the nature of partnerships. He highlights that rather than being motivated by passionate love, relationships are frequently built on compromise, value exchange, and shared interests. Relying solely on love to sustain a relationship might be disappointing because love is a transient emotion. To forge deeper bonds, people should instead concentrate on the useful parts of partnerships, such as common objectives and advantages.

Key Takeaways

- Relationships are driven by factors other than love; pragmatic concerns frequently come first.

- Long-term relationship sustainability may not be ensured by fleeting romantic love.

- Mutual gain, comprehension, and negotiation are essential components of successful partnerships.

- Healthy interactions can result from adopting a realistic perspective on relationships.

- Relationship stability may be compromised by emotional reliance.

Self-Reflection Questions

What does love mean to me in the relationships that I am in?

_____

_____

_____

_____

_____

Have I ever placed too much reliance on love to keep a relationship

going?

_____

_____

_____

_____

_____

What useful components of my connections do I value?

_____

_____

_____

_____

_____

How can I change my viewpoint such that I concentrate on how our

interactions will benefit us both?

_____

_____

_____

_____

_____

How can I get a more grounded sense of what love in relationships really is?

_____

_____

_____

_____

_____

Life-Changing Exercises

Keep a journal on your previous relationships, highlighting the relative importance of love and practical concerns.

Make a list of the qualities you think make a solid, long-lasting partnership.

Choose a relationship in your life, then evaluate the basis of that connection using mutual goals and compromise.

Talk about how to strike a balance between love and practical issues in your relationship with a partner or trustworthy friend.

Consider a relationship in which the love eventually waned and consider the reasons behind it.

CHAPTER 10: RELATIONSHIPS ARE IMPOSSIBLE FOR YOU

Chapter Summary

Taraban examines the notion that not everyone is able to build lasting relationships with everyone in this chapter. He emphasizes how crucial compatibility, common interests, and moral principles are when forming bonds with others. Putting too much stock in the idea that one can relate to anyone might result in wasted effort and disappointment. People can make deeper and more meaningful connections by concentrating their energy on relationships that are in line with their beliefs and interests by acknowledging that certain relationships might not work out.

Key Takeaways

- Mutual interest is essential for meaningful partnerships; not everyone is compatible with everyone else.

- Relationships might be more enjoyable when compatibility is the main focus.

- Making an effort to establish relationships with people who are incompatible might result in dissatisfaction and disappointment.

- Selecting the appropriate partnerships is aided by understanding one's own interests and values.

- Having quality relationships pays off more than having a lot of them.

Self-Reflection Questions

In what way do I evaluate a relationship's compatibility?

_____

_____

_____

_____

_____

Have I ever spent time in a relationship that didn't work out? If so,

what happened?

_____

_____

_____

_____

_____

Which interests and ideals do I put first when looking for connections?

_____

_____

_____

_____

_____

How can I recognize unfulfilling relationships and end them?

_____

_____

_____

_____

_____

How can I narrow down the kinds of relationships I pursue?

Life-Changing Exercises

List your interests and basic values, then use this information to assess the relationships you are in right now.

Consider failed relationships in the past and look for trends in compatibility problems.

Take part in things that interest you to meet people who share your interests.

When in a relationship that doesn't feel rewarding or compatible, practice setting limits.

Ask your friends for their opinions on the dynamics of your relationship and how compatible they think you are.

CHAPTER 11: THE BEST COURSE OF ACTION IS ALWAYS TO

Chapter Summary

Taraban talks about the idea that there's usually a better course of action when it comes to relationships. This viewpoint helps people to stay conscious of their situation and think about other ways to approach relationship dynamics. Realizing that there are always better options available might help you negotiate more skillfully and empower yourself in relationships. The secret is to maintain your flexibility and open-mindedness so that you can foster ongoing development and better interpersonal relationships.

Key Takeaways

- Relationship dynamics are always something that can be improved upon, encouraging ongoing development.

- It takes flexibility and agility to navigate relationships well.

- Acknowledging the possibility of superior choices enables people to engage in more successful negotiations.

- Relationships that are more meaningful and healthy might result from having a proactive approach.

- The ability to recognize and pursue stronger relationship moves requires self-awareness.

Self-Reflection Questions

Currently, how do I go about making decisions in my relationships?

_____

_____

_____

_____

_____

Has rigidity in my thought ever caused me to lose out on a better option?

_____

_____

_____

_____

_____

What are some tactics I may use to keep my mind open to fresh opportunities in my relationships?

_____

_____

_____

_____

_____

How can I sharpen my negotiating abilities to perhaps achieve greater results?

_____

_____

_____

_____

_____

How can I encourage an attitude of constant improvement in the way

I engage with other people?

_____

_____

_____

_____

_____

Life-Changing Exercises

Consider a recent relationship choice you made, and consider if there was a better course of action.

Have brainstorming sessions with friends or your significant other to discover fresh solutions for relationship problems.

To become more self-aware and make better relationship decisions, practice mindfulness.

Make a vision board that shows the dynamics of your ideal relationship and possible steps to achieving them.

Make a commitment to experimenting with at least one new relationship strategy per month and evaluating the results.

CHAPTER 12: RELATIONSHIPS AREN'T ACTUALLY WHAT PEOPLE DESIRE

Chapter Summary

In the last chapter, Taraban makes the argument that a lot of people don't really want partnerships in the conventional sense. Alternatively, they might look for approval, solace, or company without the dedication that accompanies genuine partnerships. This chapter challenges readers to consider why they pursue relationships and to realize that many people are more concerned with meeting their own needs than forming sincere bonds. Realizing this can help one approach relationship development more authentically by prioritizing personal fulfillment over social expectations.

Key Takeaways

- Rather of pursuing true connection, a lot of people pursue relationships for affirmation.

- Comprehending personal incentives can elucidate the dynamics of relationships.

- Sincere relationships necessitate dedication and a readiness to go beyond surface-level demands.

- Real connections might result from acknowledging the need for personal fulfillment.

- Social influences have the power to skew people's impressions of what they really desire out of relationships.

Self-Reflection Questions

What drives me to pursue partnerships, and are those drives sound ones?

_____

_____

_____

_____

_____

Have I ever chased a relationship just to feel comfortable or validated?

_____

_____

_____

_____

_____

How can I foster more meaningful relationships instead of fleeting exchanges?

_____

_____

_____

_____

_____

How do the demands of society affect the way I see relationships?

_____

_____

_____

_____

_____

How can I rethink how I approach relationships so that fulfillment and authenticity are my main priorities?

_____

_____

_____

_____

_____

Life-Changing Exercises

Write in your journal about the reasons you are looking for a relationship and assess their sincerity.

Find someone with whom you truly connect, and get in touch with them, putting genuineness ahead of superficiality.

Take part in self-discovery programs, such seminars or workshops, to examine your relationship needs and wants.

To assist you identify times when you are looking for approval instead of genuine connection, practice mindfulness.

Make a personal manifesto that will serve as a guide for your future interactions by stating your relationship-related ideals and views.

SELF-EVALUATION QUESTION

What are my guiding principles, and how do they affect the people I interact with?

_____

_____

_____

_____

_____

How well do I let people know what I need and what my boundaries are?

_____

_____

_____

_____

_____

How can I influence the dynamics of my relationships?

_____

_____

_____

_____

_____

How do I usually handle disagreements or conflicts?

_____

_____

_____

_____

_____

Am I receptive to criticism about how I behave in relationships from other people?

_____

_____

_____

_____

_____

What positive and bad trends can I see in my past relationships?

_____

_____

_____

_____

_____

In my interactions, how well do I strike a balance between my wants and those of others?

_____

_____

_____

_____

_____

Do I value being genuine above anything else in my relationships with others?

_____

_____

_____

_____

_____

How can I deal with relationships where I feel disappointed or rejected?

_____

_____

_____

_____

_____

How can I strengthen my emotional bonds with other people?

_____

_____

_____

_____

_____

Am I prepared to put in the time and energy necessary to maintain my relationships?

_____

_____

_____

_____

_____

In what ways do society norms influence my conception of the ideal relationship?

_____

_____

_____

_____

_____

How do I go about getting approval from other people, and is that a good thing?

_____

_____

_____

_____

_____

How often do I think back on why I want to pursue relationships?

_____

_____

_____

_____

_____

Which particular aspects of my interpersonal interactions do I wish to strengthen?

_____

_____

_____

_____

_____

Made in the USA
Las Vegas, NV
08 December 2024